WEST COAST

Homeland of Mist

To Lee and Sam Evans,
Bob and Ruth King,
Erin and Lueyn

WEST COAST
Homeland of Mist

CAROL EVANS
Art

BRYN KING
Introduction

Acknowledgements

For their efforts toward the production of this book, the publishing and marketing of our work, and our own personal development, we wish to sincerely thank Ken Budd, Elaine Jones, Rainer Andreesen, Linda Mitsui, Rob Fisher, Barrie Heyes, Peter Madliger, Grant Forest, Paul Lamb and staff at Hemlock Printers, Robert Jones, Yvonne and Tom Toynbee, Reggie "the Raven" Ashwell and all the great staff at Pegasus Gallery, Valerie Sawyer, Sam McDonald, Linda Collier, Sally Sunshine, Sandy Lucken, Dr. Jan McPhail and Dr. Charles Alsberg, Keith and Brenda Hiscock, Graham Sayell, Jack and Penny Crockett, Mabel, Willie and Dean Sport, J.C. Lucas, Shawani Campbell, Dan and Sue Pippin, Rose of Carmel Institute, all our wonderful staff at Dayspring Studio – Linda Smith, Sandi Wright, Mary Coombes and Heather, Gwyn and Elaine Gardam, the Baha'i Community of Saltspring, and our families.

Publisher

SummerWild
PRODUCTIONS

Producer

Mystery of Inspiration

Carol Evans happily dedicates hours of time to each of her paintings.

Carol Evans is a talented watercolorist. She is also my close companion in friendship and in marriage. As I have the double pleasure of being her husband and the promoter of her paintings, I feel fairly qualified to introduce her to you, sharing a few of the things I've grown to appreciate as I've watched her over the years at work and in life.

It is an interesting experience to live around an artist, watching painting after painting go through the various stages until completion. Sometimes I arrive home to find Carol brimming with excitement over a painting she's working on. There is hardly time to remove my coat before she calls, "Bryn, you have got to come and take a look at this!" Other times I find her agonizing and struggling over some seemingly insignificant detail. Oddly enough, what Carol finds exciting is often difficult for me to see, and what causes her concern usually looks fine to me. However, no matter what her mood, sharing the house with someone engaged in the creative process means things are never dull. And while I might not always understand or appreciate what she is attempting, it is quite a treat to be part of that process.

Carol is a person who is filled with a great love of life, and her exuberance and enthusiasm can be quite infectious.

Balancing these spirited, outgoing qualities are her gentle, contemplative nature and serious dedication to her work. I am always impressed by Carol's patience and perseverance, especially when she is at a difficult point in her painting. She'll spend hours in solitude, methodically working away, paying careful attention to each detail. When she is painting, time becomes unimportant and it seems she derives a quiet enjoyment from each stage of the process.

Time for contemplation is of great importance in Carol's life and she makes an effort to surround herself with calm and quiet. She believes it's her job as an artist to simply create a clear and peaceful environment in which the creative process can take place. This is as important to her as having paint and paper on hand and, as she says, the rest is up to "the mystery of inspiration."

Nature is a major source of inspiration for Carol, and when she's out under the open sky, watching the changing light, she seems to completely relax and feel right at home. She is an individual who is compelled to "stop and smell the roses" whenever she can. Her sense of appreciation has so influenced me that, now, I am much more conscious of the way the morning light streams through a window or filters through the trees on a foggy day.

Aware of her destiny at a very young age, Carol can't remember a time when she wasn't drawing. Her mother, Lee Evans, was a trained art teacher who encouraged her children to draw and create things with their hands, and often joined in with them. Carol still recalls her father, Sam Evans, bringing home stacks of used paper from the office, saying, "There's plenty of paper to try again, so don't be afraid to make mistakes."

Her father's job with the telephone company required

several moves throughout British Columbia for the family, and was indirectly responsible for Carol's love of nature. As her father traveled to remote parts of the province, he discovered hundreds of seldom-used back roads. He returned to some of the more beautiful places to holiday with his family, trips that nurtured the children's love for the wilderness and developed their interest in the fascinating history of the province.

After graduating from high school in Carcross, Yukon Territory, Carol remained there for a year and earned her living by painting. While there, she was befriended by a Tlingit family and was later adopted and given a native name, "Dock-rae." She learned many things from these people, including a little of their language. As members of the Bahá'í Faith, they had expanded the circle of their tribe to the horizons of the globe, including people of all cultures and traditions. Carol recalls, "Here were these people in this small, out-of-the-way village with a more advanced world vision than I had ever heard of in any modern city." Years later this experience became instrumental in her acceptance and dedication to the Bahá'í Faith.

After leaving the Yukon, Carol worked for six months in the Queen Charlotte Islands, then entered the fine arts program at the University of Victoria. The program offered a wide range of experience with various mediums, and after completing the first year it was clear that watercolor was her chosen medium. She left the university to move on toward exploring that genre on her own, and the learning process has never stopped.

When Carol began painting full time in 1981, her works proved popular with the public. Almost everything she produced sold quickly, but as an unknown artist her prices were quite low. In order to meet the demand and pay her bills, long days painting were normal, and she occasionally labored through the night. She refers to this period as "paying her tuition" for an intensive course in watercolor.

It is difficult to fit Carol into a specific slot. She is as skilled at painting people as panoramic landscapes or studies of wildlife. "I enjoy all the art forms, including abstract and impressionism, but if I try painting abstract something keeps me coming back to a particular area to put in just a little more detail. I'm trying to loosen up, but something in

The artist is at home in her studio on Saltspring Island.

Carol and her husband,
Bryn King, set aside time to enjoy their rural lifestyle.

me likes realism. What I aim for is to do it fresh and quick, but still have the realism."

Over the years, Carol has become widely known for specific "signature" qualities in her paintings. When painting a particular place or subject that has captured her interest, she tends to amplify the quality she finds attractive. In some cases it is the misty washes of an open expanse; in others the clear water of a shallow bay or stream. A quality on which people often comment is her ability to capture light. Classic examples are the sparkling reflection on the ocean's surface in "Diamond Sea," and "Crystal Cove," with the evening light glowing golden behind the island to illuminate the trees.

When depicting wildlife, Carol shows creatures as we would normally see them in their natural environment — mostly at a considerable distance. As a result, viewers often comment that a painting gives them the sense that they might have been there.

Most of the paintings featured in this book are from three major shows. For the "Saltspring Shoreline" exhibition (1985), Carol canoed around Saltspring Island to research and photograph — a visual journey along the island's shore. "The Charlottes — The Islands, The People" (1987) was a result of Carol's return to the Queen Charlotte Islands on a camping and exploration trip. "A Portrait of the Coast" (1990) was an exhibition in which she shared a collection of paintings inspired by various excursions along the British Columbia coast. We chose to include the favorites from these exhibitions.

Saltspring Island has been our home for several years, and we both enjoy the rural lifestyle it offers. We feel fortunate, indeed, to be settled in this beautiful place, and to be earning our living while working at things we love doing. Since I began publishing Carol's paintings a few years ago there has never been a dull moment. Our lives have been full and rich, the best part being that we now have a common interest in our daily work. Our greatest challenge is to find a better balance between work and periods of reflection, but despite often-busy schedules we usually manage time for a walk, or to take the canoe out for a paddle.

Carol and I refer to ourselves as "part-time parents." Erin and Lueyn, my children from a previous marriage, live most of the time on the mainland. Our relationship with them is one of guidance and friendship, which I compare to

the way my grandparents were with me when I was growing up. Carol and I treasure our time with the children and look forward to their visits. Experiencing their energy and exuberance is like holding up a magnifying glass to the world, or turning up the volume on music. They amplify many new and forgotten sounds, as well as thoughts and feelings.

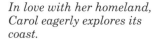

In love with her homeland, Carol eagerly explores its coast.

8

The children and Carol can often be found with their noses down at the kitchen table as they draw and color, make "things" or decorate cookies. There is such an atmosphere of fun it seems there are three kids at play.

Sharing my life with Carol has been — and continues to be — an enriching experience. I never cease to marvel at the scenes that materialize as her paintings develop: an exquisite shell beach at sunrise, a shallow stream meandering through a field of wild flowers; a sunlit passage leading out to the ocean and beyond. As I watch, I often wonder where it will all lead — what her paintings will look like in the future and how she will use her talent. But I suppose that must all be left up to "the mystery of inspiration." In the meantime, I hope you will enjoy Carol's paintings as much as I do.

–Bryn King

An evening paddle soothes the spirit and provides inspiration.

the art of

CAROL EVANS

Lessons
Hidden in Every Leaf

The young woman sat for a long time in deep contemplation, soaking up the sounds and solace of the river, letting it run through her silence.

(Watercolor, 28"x 9", September 1991)

Carmanah's River

The rainforest crowds right to the shore, still and immense, the constant flow of the river its life-giving artery.

(Watercolor, 10^{7}/$_{8}$"x 28", September 1991)

*"In the wild places, more than anywhere else,
I feel closest to the source of my existence."*

Trails of Light

It's a game to walk upstream in the shallows of the river and ride the current down in the deep channel near the shore. As they make their way up, these girls, illumined in the afternoon sun, create brilliant trails of light.

(Watercolor, 8½"x 20⅜", June 1990; published as a limited edition March 1991)

Bathing in Light

The river provides an invigorating
refuge from the summer's heat;
the people, the water, the trees,
all shimmer in the sunlight.

(Watercolor, 11"x 28", June 1990)

*"During this brief walk upon the earth,
nature and her secrets, her brilliance and diversity,
are continual sources of renewal and inspiration."*

Gabriola

On late summer evenings,
we'd take a picnic and sit on
the sandstone, still warm
from the sun, to watch
the moon rise.

(Watercolor, 20"x 28", June 1991;
published as a limited edition
November 1991)

Jubilation

Delight on a summer's afternoon.

(Watercolor, 19$\frac{1}{2}$"x 12$\frac{7}{8}$, August 1992)

Crystal Cove Morning

The overnight high tide smoothed the sand and left a quiet pool in the morning.

(Watercolor, 28"x 20", February 1990; published as a limited edition January 1991)

*"Being near the ocean, its force
and its energy, has a way of sweeping you clean,
just as it sweeps the beach clean."*

**Gulls
at the Tideline**
Their whiteness
reflects the rosy glow
of sunrise, while
the shining sand
reflects them.

(Watercolor,
12⅝"x 19⅝",
June 1990)

Crystal Cove

Evening sunlight spills in behind the island,
silhouetting the trees.
(Watercolor, 20"x 27⁷/₈", March 1989)

First Light on Third Sister Island

The morning light bathes all in it's path,
gradually warming the stones.

(Watercolor, 11"x 19", August 1985)

Winter Sun

December 24th on Mackenzie Beach: riding bikes
on the hard-packed sand, children play according
to the tide's time.

(Watercolor, 9¹/2"x 27", August 1990)

*"The constantly changing tides
bring us great wealth from the sea.
We must never take it for granted."*

Clam Digger

Clam digging on a
fog-shrouded morning at Rose Spit.

(Watercolor, 12¹/₂"x 19", February 1987)

Seaweed Gathering

The spring tides wash seaweed up in
abundance and many of us collect it for
our gardens. The vibrant green of the
back-lit seaweed, combined with Sally's
grace, caught my eye.

(Watercolor, 19"x 12¹/₂", November 1989;
published as a limited edition March 1990)

Friends

Three friends sit together,
enjoying the sun,
each in his own way.

(Watercolor, 16"x 28", October 1988)

Respect

At the ragged edge of the land,
surrounded by the power of the ocean,
a young man stands watching.

(Watercolor, 20¼"x 27¼", January 1992)

Contrasts

Water crashes onto the sand, filling the air
with a tumultuous roar. It rushes up the
beach, wave after wave, regular as a
heartbeat. Only a few feet away, tide pools
like perfect Japanese gardens lie undisturbed
until the rising tide floods them once again.

(Watercolor, 20½"x 28", October 1989;
 published as a limited edition January 1990)

Mudge and Link

Where these two islands meet, the Pacific seems to be at its gentlest. Storms do venture in here sometimes, but on a peaceful day, when the tide rises over the white shell sand, there is nothing more mesmerizing than that dancing water.

(Watercolor, 20"x 28", December 1989; published as a limited edition May 1990)

Tidepool

The headlands at Botanical Beach, warmly lit in the afternoon sun, cast reflections across a tidepool where another beauty lies beneath the surface of the water.

(Watercolor, 27"x 20", May 1988; published as a limited edition September 1988)

Tide's Garden

In this amazing, self-contained little world, creatures sway gracefully in the current or dart and flash.

(Watercolor, 12¹/₂"x 20", May 1988)

*"Beyond the forest,
beneath the surface,
there is a fascinating world
unnoticed by many."*

Long Harbor Point

In the summer heat, there is
a magical quality about this point.

(Watercolor, 20"x 13", April 1990)

Loon in Seabright Bay

Against the background of cool green,
the loon appears to attract light to itself
as it ruffles the water with its wings.

(Watercolor, 20$\frac{1}{8}$"x 27$\frac{7}{8}$", September 1990)

"What a glorious part of the world is that perpetually changing boundary where the land meets the sea."

Homeward Flight

As the line of swans headed towards
their home in the harbor, we could hear
the rhythmic whisper of their wings
parting the air.

(Watercolor, 7¹/₈"x 25¹/₄", April 1989;
published as a limited edition June 1989)

Swans in Fulford Harbor

Heads bowed and feathers glowing
in the morning light, these swans
grace the harbor.

(Watercolor, 19"x 26", August 1987)

"Water reflects the sky, it's companion, in every changing mood."

Diamond Sea

The currents in the channel between the islands dance with light on this bright summer day.

(Watercolor, 20"x 28", January 1988; published as a limited edition November 1988)

Dawn

The early sounds of activity on the water begin at dawn's first light.

(Watercolor, 20"x 27", March 1988)

The Old Boathouse

Having weathered many seasons, the old boathouse still provides shelter.

(Watercolor, 12"x 19", September 1985)

Little Rowboat

The little boat rests on a quiet beach, bathed in the long rays of the evening sun.

(Watercolor, 12"x 20", July 1990; published as a limited edition September 1991)

Evening Port of Call

I camped here the first night on my journey around Saltspring Island. My strongest recollection is of the warmth of the beach and the path after a long day of sun.

(Watercolor, 23"x 18", August 1985)

Dawn at Walker Hook

In the blue silence of early morning,
the air is still and the water laps gently
at the shore.

(Watercolor, 12"x 19", August 1985)

August Moon

Silent as the moon, herons fly past the shores of Russell Island in the half-light of evening.

(Watercolor, 12⁷/₈"x 20¹/₂", August 1990; published as a limited edition August 1992)

Heron in the Afternoon

A great blue heron stands motionless, focused and waiting, while all around is movement and light.

(Watercolor, 13"x 19³/₄", February 1991)

Homeland of Mist

The mist, always shifting and changing, momentarily hangs over
the headlands as a pair of eagles fly above the tidal flats.

(Watercolor, 20¹/₄"x 27⁷/₈", May 1990; published as a limited edition November 1990)

*"We need to use
the eagle's qualities
of strength and
far-sighted vision
to secure its homeland
and our own."*

Circling the River

Continually tumbling, the river
spills past the forest, rushing towards
the sea, watched, ever watched,
by a circling eagle.

(Watercolor, 28"x 20", May 1991;
published as a limited edition July 1992)

Princess Louisa Inlet

Two eagles wing their way across
the mist-shrouded inlet just after
the last spring snowfall.

(Watercolor, 20"x 28", November 1988;
published as a limited edition May 1989)

Eagle at Tow Hill

The whispered stroke of wind
through feathers emerges
from the stillness of the forest.

(Watercolor, 20"x 27", February 1987;
Published as a limited edition June 1987)

Unity in Diversity

A native friend told us that when you see
cormorants and seals together like this
it means there are a lot of fish in the area.

(Watercolor, 20"x 28", October 1988;
published as a limited edition March 1989)

*"I'm always amazed at
how close these creatures live to the borders
of our human environment."*

Newborn Harbor Seal

When I canoed past, the mother
jumped into the water,
leaving her baby camouflaged
among the rocks. It would have
been well hidden except for its
occasional hoarse cry.

(Watercolor, 12½"x 19", September 1985)

Heading into Jervis Inlet

Heavily veiled in fog,
steep mountainous walls
dwarf even the whales.

(Watercolor, triptych, September 1990)
[1] Sky 7^{11}/$_{16}$"x 11"
[2] Whales 9^{3}/$_{16}$"x 11"
[3] Narrows 20^{3}/$_{16}$"x 16^{1}/$_{8}$"

Canoe Ceremony

Drums speak and voices chant in a ceremony
celebrating a community,
honoring a culture, at the launching of
a very special canoe.

(Watercolor, 18"x 27", July 1987)

Silent Village

Over the centuries, many things have
happened at this place: some powerful,
momentous; others simple, insignificant.
The poles stand quiet in the wind, but
walking among them you do not feel alone.

(Watercolor, 20"x 28", March 1987)

"Passed on from generation to generation,
the enduring culture of the First Peoples
is a tribute to their inner strength of spirit."

The Silent Ones

A fallen pole returns to the earth.

(Watercolor, 20½"x 28", January 1990)

Spirit of the Ancients

Master Haida artists carved these poles from cedar in a different age. Despite years of fierce winds and rain, they continue to have a powerful spiritual presence.

(Watercolor, 27"x 20", February 1987; published as a limited edition April 1987)

Between Earth and Sky

If you spend any time looking at
the trees in Carmanah Valley,
you start to recognize them as
individuals with their own
identifiable characteristics.
It was this individual quality
I wanted to portray. I painted
them as old people, ancestors,
seeing native characteristics in
their connection to the earth.
They seemed to be reaching,
embracing the sky.

(Watercolor, 28"x 20½", August 1989;
published as a limited edition
November 1989)

The Power and the Mystery

Walking through thick overgrown forest,
we found, hidden among the trees,
the tallest, most magnificent Haida pole
I have ever seen. The strength and authority
staring out through those eyes
was so powerful you could almost feel it.

(Watercolor, 20"x 12¹/₂", October 1990;
published as a limited edition May 1991)

June Meadow

The children amble through the meadow;
after the spring rains, it is fresh and green,
wild flowers scattered like brightly
colored jewels.

(Watercolor, 19$^7/_8$"x 27$^5/_8$", June 1992)

*"I would say the reason so many of us
spend long hours alone, quietly trying
to paint the things we see and feel,
is because we are completely enraptured
by the beauty and depth of it all."*

Fireweed on the Beach

Beyond the reach of the sea,
fireweed flourishes amongst the driftwood.

(Watercolor, 13"x 9½", September 1985)

"At times this coast is a place of dazzling light. At times it offers solace. At times it is the abode of mystery. To me it is a sacred strand linking the land to the sea, fragile yet powerful."

—*Carol Evans*

Kingfishers' Perch

Where water and forest meet
and light filters through the trees,
they await opportunity.

(Watercolor, 12¼"x 20", October 1985)

Passage through the Rocks

Carved by the surging tides, this passage
leads irresistibly from the quiet of the
dense rainforest, out to the open Pacific.

(Watercolor, 20¹/₁₆"x 27⁷/₈", July 1992;
published as a limited edition October 1992)

Index of Images

CANADIAN CATALOGING IN PUBLICATION DATA

Evans, Carol
    West Coast, homeland of mist

    Includes index
    --ISBN 0-9696135-1-2 (bound)
    --ISBN 0-9696135-0-4 (pbk)

1. Evans, Carol--Criticism and interpretation.
2. Pacific Coast (B.C.) in art. I. Title.
ND1843.I92A4 1992.   759.11   C92-091608-2

Ancillary Products

To order the Collector's Edition or autographed hardcover copies of this book, or for information regarding limited edition prints, please contact:

    Dayspring Studio
    R.R. #1, Fulford Harbor, B.C.
    Canada V0S 1C0
    Phone/Fax: (604) 653-4479

Printed on recycled paper.
Printed in Canada.

PRODUCTION CREDITS:

Executive Producer: Bryn King
Producer: Ken Budd
Designers: Ken Budd, Bryn King & Carol Evans
Layout Artist: Rainer Andreesen
Editors: Elaine Jones & Robert H. Jones
Typesetters: Profile Design Ltd., Vancouver
Color Separator & Printer:
    Hemlock Printers Ltd., Burnaby
Binders: North-West Book Co. Ltd., Surrey
    & Coast Trade Bindery, Vancouver

Publisher:

Dayspring Studio
R.R. #1, Fulford Harbor, B.C.
Canada V0S 1C0
Phone/Fax: (604) 653-4479

Producer:

SummerWild Productions
#2202-1275 Pacific Street,
Vancouver, B.C. V6E 1T6
Phone/Fax: (604) 681-0015

Distributor:

Raincoast Books
112 East 3rd Avenue,
Vancouver, B.C. V5T 1C8
Phone: (604) 873-6581
Fax: (604) 874-2711